Original title:
Tasting Nectar

Copyright © 2025 Creative Arts Management OÜ
All rights reserved.

Author: Mariana Leclair
ISBN HARDBACK: 978-1-80586-261-1
ISBN PAPERBACK: 978-1-80586-733-3

Sweetness Unveiled in the Garden

In a garden, bees do dance,
Chasing scents, they take a chance.
Petals giggle, colors bright,
Buzzing jokes in morning light.

Lemon drops on bumble's feet,
While daisies laugh at bees they meet.
Fruit so ripe, it wears a grin,
Let the tasting games begin!

The Aroma of Blossoms Unleashed

Whiffs of laughter fill the air,
A bloom decides to dye its hair.
Minty whispers tease the breeze,
'Taste me first!' says the sweet peas!

Pollen parties on a stem,
Nature's way of saying: 'Hymn!'
A banquet set on grassy beds,
Witty flowers, silly threads.

Indulgences in a Meadow's Embrace

In the meadow, joy's at play,
Caterpillars munch all day.
Worms in sun hats sing a tune,
While daisies wink and dance at noon.

Berries blush and giggle loud,
Underneath a fluffy cloud.
Cheeky flavors take their chance,
In this reckless summer dance.

Sun-Kissed Delicacies

Golden rays bring smiles anew,
Glorious fruits share what they do.
Ricochet of flavors bright,
Sun-kissed wonders, pure delight!

Honey drips from flowers' kiss,
Each drop holds a taste of bliss.
Sipping sunshine, laughter reels,
Nature's way of serving meals.

Petals and Pleasures

Butterflies giggle with glee,
As they sip from cups of tea.
Bees buzzing, a comic crew,
Pollinating just for you.

Flowers dance in vibrant hues,
Sprinkling laughter, no time to snooze.
In gardens where joy takes flight,
Every bloom a silly sight!

Eden's Elixir

In the garden of jest and cheer,
Fruits hang low with a grin, oh dear!
A sip of vines, a splash of fun,
Chasing shadows on the run.

Grapes insist they're quite refined,
But squeeze too hard, they lose their mind.
Juice flies up, a comedic show,
Leftovers squished on toes below!

Sweet Drops of Memory

Sticky fingers and silly faces,
Chasing down those sweet embraces.
Lemonade laughs on a sunny day,
Too much fun to fade away!

Giggles splatter, lemon zest,
Citrus jokes are simply the best!
A memory forms with each sweet lick,
Oh the joy – and that was quick!

Gourmet Reveries

Whisking dreams with a dash of flair,
Cakes that dance in midair!
Chocolate swirls, a twirly treat,
Desserts that tickle your hungry feet.

Cookies joke with each crumbling bite,
As sugar sprinkles take flight.
Each dish a comedy parade,
In this feast, fun won't fade!

Caress of the Softest Sweets

A cupcake walked with charm and flair,
Its frosting giggled, light as air.
"Take a bite, it's such a thrill!"
The cherry on top gave a cheeky spill.

Sugar sprinkles danced with glee,
Marshmallows puffed up, oh so free.
"Let's have a party, just us treats!"
They rolled in laughter, sweets with feats.

Nectar of Celestial Laughter

A jelly bean fell from the sky,
It bounced on clouds, oh my, oh my!
With each crack, a giggle arose,
"Who knew we could dance in yellow shoes?"

Chocolate bars in a comical race,
Trying to win the sticky face.
"I tripped on caramel, what a mess!"
But sticky laughter won the contest.

Whispers of Sweetness

Candy canes had a secret plan,
To make a world of sugar fans.
They whispered softly, behind the jars,
"Let's tickle noses with our sugary stars!"

Gumdrops told tales in a gooey style,
Made everyone chuckle for a while.
"But watch the licorice, it's quite sly,"
"It'll sneak up, oh my, oh my!"

The Honeyed Breeze

In a land where honey bees sing,
The air was thick with a sweet fling.
Bumblebees buzzing, bees in a twist,
"Careful now, don't get on our list!"

Pollen parachutes drifted by,
Tickling noses, oh me, oh my!
"Let's have a race, you buttercup!"
With laughter brewing in every cup.

Savoring the Silk of Petals

In gardens where the bees do buzz,
A hint of sweetness stirs the fuzz.
I took a sip from flower's dress,
And woke up feeling quite a mess.

My friends all laughed, I spilled it wide,
The golden drop, my pride and glide.
They offered me a napkin quick,
But I just danced, that was my trick.

Nectarine Serenade

Oh, juicy fruits hang from the trees,
I play the fool, I catch the breeze.
A squirt, a splash, it drips like rain,
I lick my lips, this moment's gain.

With every bite, I make a mess,
My shirt now wears a sticky dress.
I serenade the bloated ants,
While dancing in my fruit-filled pants.

Morsels of Morning Bliss

Sunrise beams through my window wide,
I smile at toast, my breakfast guide.
But when I spread the jam so bold,
It's like a slip on buttered gold!

My toast's a canvas, oh what fun!
With every swipe, I just can't run.
The crumbs confetti on my lap,
Living it up, a tasty nap!

The Dance of Juicy Sunbeams

In pools of light, the fruit does spark,
I twirl around, and miss my mark.
A dance with berries, ripe and round,
A slippery fate is what I found.

With every step, I trip and glide,
The juicy drops go sliding wide.
I laugh and slip, what can I say?
Tomorrow's dance, I'll plan the fray.

A Taste of Imagination

In a land where gumdrops grow,
Creatures dance, putting on a show.
With candy rain and chocolate streams,
The world is sweeter than your dreams.

Silly mice wear hats of blue,
Sipping tea made from berry dew.
They giggle as they jump and play,
In a land where joy won't fade away.

Fluffy clouds like cotton candy,
Twist and turn, oh so dandy.
Lollipops grow on trees so tall,
Each bite's a echoing sugar call.

Throw confetti made of sprinkles,
Watch as laughter sweetly twinkles.
Take a bite and share a grin,
Let the fun and flavor begin!

Drenched in Sunshine

Lemonade rivers flow with glee,
Winking frogs hold a jubilee.
Jumping jellies bounce so high,
Chasing shadows beneath the sky.

Sundaes melt in playful glares,
While butterflies weave through chairs.
Sunshine spills like syrup sweet,
Kites dance high, with joy they greet.

Balloons float with a pop and spin,
As giggles play like music in.
Each sip a burst of happy cheer,
Underneath the sky so clear.

Sorbet smiles on everyone's face,
In this dreamy, silly place.
Forget your worries, have a blast,
In the glow where fun is cast!

The Art of Sweetness

A painter's brush dips in syrup bliss,
Creating joy with every swish.
Gummy bears in a vivid hue,
Dancing, twirling just for you.

Caramel rivers, oh so thick,
Misty fog of chocolate slick.
The canvas shows a world so bright,
Sugar-coated dreams take flight.

Whipped cream clouds float delightfully,
In a world that's oh-so-bubbly.
Grab a spoon, dig in with glee,
What a sight, just wait and see!

Laughter echoes, a melody sweet,
With every color, life's a treat.
Artful bites, both fun and bold,
A masterpiece that never grows old!

Sugared Whispers

Syrupy secrets float in air,
Tickling noses here and there.
Sugary sighs of marshmallow fluff,
Soft giggles, we can't get enough.

Choco-chums in a candy patch,
Playing hide-and-seek with a match.
Lollipop trees sway with the breeze,
Whispering softly through the leaves.

Peppermint dreams swirl around,
As jellybeans smile, hopping bound.
Each bite is a giggle in disguise,
Sweets that twinkle in eager eyes.

Bubbles burst with fruity cheer,
In a whimsical land of no fear.
Let's laugh and snack, oh what a fuss,
In the world of whispers, just for us!

Ambrosia's Embrace

In a jar marked 'Do Not Touch',
A sweetness made for lunch,
Bees buzz around in queue,
Wondering what they ought to chew.

With a wink and a sticky hand,
I dip my spoon, oh isn't it grand?
It slips and slides, a sugar dance,
A drizzle leads to a clumsy chance.

My fingers trace a golden streak,
In my mouth, a burst, unique.
Friends laugh as I make a mess,
Chasing sweetness, I confess!

The floor is sticky, the laughs are loud,
I wear the goo like a proud shroud,
Ambrosia drips from every face,
Oh, what a tasty, messy race!

Flavor of Sunlit Mornings

With dawn's light comes a jar,
Full of sunshine, oh so far,
I spread it thick on toast, you see,
Goodness dripping, just for me.

My breakfast plate, a golden hue,
In one bite, a blissful view,
Forks fall and laughter flies,
As I devour, oh how time flies.

Sipping juice with a splash of cheer,
Wearing stickiness, never fear,
Neighbors peek and giggle, too,
As I slip and slide right out of the view.

Morning giggles, messes await,
A sweet banquet, isn't it great?
Sunlit laughter fills the air,
With each bite, life's beyond compare!

The Golden Liquid

In a bottle marked 'Elixir of Fun',
I cracked it open, oh what a run!
My bread is waiting, knife in hand,
A pour that makes my taste buds grand.

The moment it lands, a joyful splash,
I laugh and giggle, let's make a stash!
My fingers slip, the bottle sways,
What a mess on these bright sunny days!

Friends come over, their faces gleam,
As we dive into our sweet, sticky dream,
A golden river flows like wine,
We toast with cheers, oh it's divine!

In sticky chaos, we find delight,
As laughter echoes, day turns to night,
With each spoonful, our worries flee,
And my kitchen's a joy, come taste with me!

Essence of Delight

From blossoms sweet, they took the best,
A jar of giggles, let's put it to test,
I dipped my finger, oh what a sight,
The essence of delight, pure and bright.

Spreading joy on muffins stacked,
The gooey sweetness has me racked,
It jumps and hops like a playful clown,
On my chin, it drips and frowns.

Laughter spilled with every bite,
My friends join in, what a delight,
We slip and slide, there's no regret,
With each big laugh, more we beget.

As the sun sets, we dance and twirl,
In the sticky mess, our laughter swirls,
The essence of joy is hard to define,
But trust me, it's best when we dine!

Harvest of Warmth

In the garden where bees plot,
Honey spills like a sugary trot.
Jars lined up with a twist of fate,
Sweetness served on a wobbly plate.

Lemon zest meets playful cheer,
Straws that dance while sipping beer.
A waft of joy, it's all a game,
Little bugs join in the fame.

Each drop brings a giggle or two,
Sticky fingers in shades of dew.
Laughter bubbles in the bright sun,
Harvest season? Oh, what fun!

Underneath the peachy trees,
Smiles abound with buzzing bees.
Sunshine's warmth, a playful tease,
Gather 'round, a feast, if you please!

Cascading Elixirs

From the fountain of fruity bliss,
A splash of sweetness, can't resist!
Bubbles rise in a giddy whirl,
Cup in hand, watch the magic swirl.

Chocolate rivers flow like dreams,
Strawberries dance in creamy streams.
Sips that tickle, giggles spin,
Every slurp a win-win grin.

Wobble cups on a sunny deck,
Pour a splash, what the heck!?
A fizzing burst, a wild chase,
Friends all join in the sweet embrace.

Tongue-tied tales in the summer heat,
With every sip, we can't be beat.
Cascading flavors, joy unleashed,
Life's a party, we're all quite pleased!

A Symphony of Sweets

Truffles playing hide and seek,
In chocolate lands, the flavors speak.
Fudge and caramel on parade,
Every bite a joyful escapade.

Pop rocks dance in fizzy rows,
Creating music as each one glows.
Lollipops singing tunes so bright,
Sugary laughter, pure delight.

Cotton candy clouds afloat,
Giggles burst, a sweet little boat.
Marshmallows marsh as we all munch,
Joy served warm, a sugary crunch.

Syrup flows like a happy stream,
Each bite comes with a tasty dream.
Life's a concert of candy treats,
Where fun and flavor intertwine sweetly beats.

Petals in the Breeze

In a meadow, laughter flies,
Petals swirl like tasty pies.
Jelly beans scatter in the sun,
Chasing shadows, oh what fun!

Bubblegum blossoms fill the air,
Sticky wonders everywhere.
Candy corn on a wind-blown stroll,
A picnic spread to tickle the soul.

Frolic in the playful hues,
Sipping nectar from bright green views.
With friends beside, a quirky blend,
Joyful echoes that never end.

Nature's laughter in the breeze,
Sharing sweets with such great ease.
Petal power, let's believe,
In a world where fun won't leave!

Sweet Elixirs of Dawn

The bee wears a tiny crown,
Buzzing round, never a frown.
With every drop, it does declare,
"Hey, humans, come have a share!"

From flowers bright, they make their art,
A sticky treat, a sugary heart.
Spilled on toast or in a tea,
It rivals all things sweet, you see!

They dance like bliss in the sun's embrace,
With sticky legs, they hold their place.
A smear on pancakes, what a delight,
Who knew breakfast could take flight?

So lift a spoon to those little guys,
Creating joy and goofy sighs.
For in their work, fun swirls around,
As morning's laughter does abound!

The Flutter of Flavor

The hummingbirds chase a sugary thrill,
With tiny beaks, they sip and chill.
In the garden, they take a dive,
And create a buzz, oh, how they thrive!

The daisies smile, the roses wink,
As nectar drips, they share a drink.
The butterflies join with dips and dives,
In this sweet world, nobody jives!

A sippy straw for every bloom,
Sipping away, they clear the room.
"Who needs a party? We've got zeal!"
Forget the punch, let's keep it real!

In every flutter, a giggle's found,
Nature's bar is always around.
So let's toast with laughter and cheer,
To the wacky wonders that bring us near!

Sipping the Sun

A sunbeam caught in liquid gold,
Every drop a story told.
People line up for a taste,
But nature's treats, they can't waste!

Sticky fingers, happy grins,
Everyone wants to join the spins.
With each sip, we sing and sway,
Good vibes only—come what may!

Drop by drop, it's quite a scene,
As bees buzz like a charming machine.
Elixirs sweet like a summer's day,
Who knew bingeing on fun was the way?

So sip deeply and laugh out loud,
Join the nectar-loving crowd.
With sunshine packed in every jar,
This is the best time, let's raise a star!

Essence of Floral Whispers

In gardens where laughter takes a stroll,
Petals peek out, playing their role.
"Just a sip, don't be so shy!"
The flowers giggle, oh my, oh my!

With honey drips, the tea gets sweet,
A party in a cup, oh what a treat!
Cupcakes and cookies line the way,
"Come one, come all, let's enjoy the fray!"

Jars filled to the brim, what a sight,
Every color, every flavor, just right.
Friends all gather, what a swish,
Nectar dreams in every sip and swish!

So raise your glasses, make a toast,
To floral whispers we love the most.
In every giggle, in every cheer,
Let's celebrate fun, it's finally here!

The Essence of Joy

In a garden of flavors, I met a bee,
She winked and buzzed, 'Come laugh with me!'
We danced on petals, twirled in delight,
Sipping sunshine till the fall of night.

A plump little fruit rolled down the lane,
It tripped on a rock and shouted, 'Oh, plain!'
But with a chuckle, I knew its secret,
Sweetness awaits under every bleak bit.

Bubbles popped in a sparkling drink,
We'd giggle and spill, and not even think!
With each silly sip, our worries took flight,
We laughed till we dropped, oh what a night!

A pickle in gloves tried to join in the fun,
But slipped on a grape – oh, what a run!
The joy of the moment, forever will stay,
In this feast of laughter, come join the play!

Ageless Sweets

A chocolate fudge with a wink so sweet,
Said, 'Join the party! Grab a seat!'
The jellybeans jumped, a colorful crew,
Inviting all folks for a wild rendezvous.

An old cookie grinned, with a crumbly voice,
'Life's short,' it said, 'make a tasty choice!'
With sprinkles of mischief and frosting of cheer,
We munched and we giggled, forgetting our fear.

A candy cane danced, with a jolly old jive,
Saying, 'With flavors like these, you'll feel so alive!'
Lollipops sang songs of sugary glee,
In a merry parade, come taste life with me!

But then came the pie, with a crust made of dreams,
Declared, 'I'm the champion of sweet, it seems!'
Yet a cheeky tart whispered, 'There's more to explore!'
We chewed through the night, asking, 'Is there ever a bore?'

Enchanted Sips

In a land where the giggles grew over the edge,
A tea party bloomed near a whimsical hedge.
With teacups that danced and spoons that could sing,
We sipped all the laughter, oh what joy it did bring!

The honey dripped down with a comical flair,
As bees in tuxedos buzzed round with a care.
'Careful now!' one shouted, 'Don't spill the fun!'
We laughed as it dribbled, our madness begun.

Pickles would prance, quite proud of the show,
Waving their brine in a salty ballet flow.
But happily sipping zesty lemonade,
We all raised our glasses, our worries would fade.

The juice from the fruits started jiving around,
With flavors so nutty, they'd never be found.
Each sip was a giggle, a burst of pure bliss,
In this enchanted realm, who could ever resist?

Nectarine Dreams

In the garden, I took a bite,
Juice flew left, a sticky fight.
Worms think they're in a race,
While I'm just smearing my face.

Bees buzz by, oh what a tease,
Chasing sweetness like a breeze.
I pranced as if I might just dance,
But tripped over my own pants.

Savoring the Unseen

Peeking under every leaf,
Found a snack that brought me grief.
One sip had me in a whirl,
Sticky hands, oh what a swirl!

Cherries rolled, escaped the bowl,
Stuck to shoes, they reached their goal.
Giggling kids, they start to shout,
"Who's the fool that spilled it out?"

Beads of Joy

Sour stains on my new shirt,
The fruit was sweet, but oh the hurt!
Nibbles turn to clumsy slips,
Lemonade splashed from my lips.

Lemon drops become a game,
Fruits are laughing, feel no shame.
Citrus jests, they play it cool,
As I declare, "I'm such a fool!"

The Lure of Sugared Vines

Vines entwined with a secret grin,
Enticing flavors, oh where to begin?
Berries flop, like clowns on stage,
Each burst of joy a fruit-filled rage.

Caught in a tangle, I'm entwined,
Licking fingers, oh what a find!
Nature's candy, such a tease,
While I'm giggling, lost at ease.

Tastebuds Dance

A drip of sweetness, oh what bliss,
My mouth's a circus, can't resist,
Flavors twirl, they jump, they spin,
A giggle slips out, let the feast begin!

Lemon makes me pucker, oh what a tease,
While mango winks, brings me to my knees,
Strawberries burst, a comedy show,
Each bite's a punchline, oh don't you know?

Lollipop raindrops fall from the sky,
Dancing on tongues, oh my, oh my!
Gelato dreams, in the summer sun,
A frosty giggle, oh this is fun!

Onward we go, flavor parade,
With whipped cream clouds, we're unafraid,
The joy we find in every taste,
Let this silly feast never go to waste!

Juice of the Gods

I've mixed a potion, oh what a sight,
Colors bouncing, pure delight,
Grapes do the cha-cha, berries hop,
Why are the cherries sporting a mop?

Oranges giggle, such juicy jest,
Pineapples pirouette, they're the best,
Coconuts roll, with laughter they pour,
In my glass, a sweet folklore!

Fruits in a blender, a raucous show,
Spin and whirl, watch them go!
A sprinkle of humor, a zest of cheer,
In every drop, my smile is sheer!

So raise your glass, let's toast to fun,
A drink for everyone, let the party run,
Sip by sip, we giggle more,
With juice from the heavens, who could ask for more?

Abundance in a Spoon

Scoop me up some laughter, oh what a treat,
A mountain of flavors piled high and neat,
Ice cream giggles as it melts away,
A silly dessert that wants to play!

Chocolate swirls, a wild ride,
Marshmallows wave, with a fluffy glide,
Sprinkles jump in, a colorful cheer,
This spoonful of joy brings everyone near!

A dance of flavors, a vibrant scene,
Funny faces made by the whipped cream,
Every scoop's a chuckle, laughter's the key,
Dig in my friend, it's fun, you'll see!

So let's embrace this simple delight,
With every bite, we laugh out loud, right?
This spoonful of magic, oh what a boon,
In each little morsel, happiness balloons!

Honeyed Moonlight

Under the stars, a sweet serenade,
Buzzing bees dance, in twilight parade,
Drizzled sweetness, a sticky swirl,
As giggles abound, let the laughter twirl!

Spoons of sunshine, oh what a sight,
Golden nectar glows in the night,
A dip and a dart, can't help but smile,
As we savor the magic, just for a while!

biscuits crunching, slathered with glee,
Honeycombs whisper, come join the spree,
A honey pot overflows, bursting bright,
Each taste a tickle, pure and light!

So let's indulge in this sweet delight,
With giggles and chuckles glowing so bright,
In the moon's warm glow, let's joyously swoon,
As we revel together with the honeyed moon!

Ripened Moments

A juicy blob slips from my hands,
Like trying to catch a slippery band.
Laughter echoes in the air,
As squishy fruit makes a hilarious flare.

Biting into a peach, it's quite the dance,
Juice drips down—oh, what a chance!
My shirt a canvas of sticky delight,
Who knew fruit could bring such a sight?

A cherry plops right on my nose,
As laughter erupts, and the fun just grows.
I look ridiculous, a fruit-fatality,
But in this moment, I find pure reality.

These ripened moments, a playful spree,
Turning spills into sweet jubilee.
Each mishap a giggle, a fond retreat,
Banana peels cannot be beat!

The Alchemy of Flavor

In a kitchen bubbling with chaos and cheer,
I stir the pot, maybe something will appear.
Grapes tumble, rolling around with glee,
"Hey, watch out!" I yell, as they go free.

There's a dash of whimsy, a sprinkle of fun,
Goosebumps tickle as the flavors run.
I taste the rainbow, it makes me grin,
Who knew mixing marshmallows could lead to a win?

Tasting minty explosions, oh what a ride,
Combining pickles with pudding, I can't hide.
Friends gather round, a culinary show,
With each mix-up, we share a sweet glow.

Laughter erupts, oh, the things we create,
Flavors collide, oh, isn't that fate?
In this wild kitchen, joy is the flavor,
And every odd bite becomes our savior!

Drunken by Delight

Sipping nectar, ah, for goodness sake,
Stumbling on sweetness, what a wild quake!
With every sip, my head starts to swirl,
Like candy-flavored whirls in a playful twirl.

In my cup, a concoction so bright,
Dazzling colors, a sugary sight.
One little sip, oh, it's pure glee,
Giggles explode, as I climb a tree!

Fruit-fueled shenanigans, I must confess,
Berries bounce around, causing a mess.
A dragonfruit winks as it rolls by,
"Catch me if you can!" it dares with a sigh.

Drunken by delight, laughter unfolds,
These fruity frolics are pure gold.
With every spill, every laugh, oh, so bright,
Let's juggle our joy and dance through the night!

Symphony of Flavors

In the orchard of giggles, the fruits sing loud,
A symphony of flavors, oh, isn't it proud?
Melons conduct with a slippery sway,
While oranges dance, come out to play.

A banana solo, sweet as can be,
Harmonizing with apples, oh, such a spree.
Peaches join in, with a soft, juicy tone,
Creating a melody that's all our own.

Pineapple jingles, in rhythms so bright,
Creating a chorus, what a hilarious sight!
Mangoes add drums, with a boisterous beat,
As berries join in, we all feel the heat.

This fruity orchestra, a joy to behold,
Bringing smiles and giggles, stories retold.
In the laughter of flavors, together we soar,
A symphony of joy that we can't ignore!

The Sweetest Harmony

In a jar, oh what a sight,
Sticky fingers, sweet delight,
Buzzing bees dance here and there,
Caught in sugar-coated snare.

Spilling sweetness on my shirt,
A sticky mess, my dessert hunt,
Licking lips, a happy grin,
Who knew this jar could cause such din?

Honey drips and laughter flies,
As we swallow gooey pies,
With each bite, a giggle grows,
Life's absurdity just shows.

Chasing sweetness with my spoon,
Like a bee that sings a tune,
Buzzing with a joyful glee,
Nature's candy's made for me!

Romantic Essence

Underneath the moon's soft glow,
Spills our lover's sticky flow,
Knocked over jars, oh what a mess,
Kissed by sweetness, I confess.

We dance, we drip, we giggle loud,
Flavors mixed, like love unbowed,
Taste explosions in the air,
Sticky kisses everywhere!

"Try my jam!" you cheekily boast,
A toast to sticky affairs we toast,
Yet your aim's a tad off base,
Now there's marmalade on your face!

Pass the syrup, don't be shy,
We'll spoon together, oh, my!
Who knew love could be so sweet?
Tastier still than any treat!

Feast of the Senses

Gather round, the feast begins,
With flavors bold, we crack our grins,
Dipping fruits in golden glue,
Feeling silly, just me and you.

Spoons collide with sugary crash,
Laughter echoes with each splash,
Floating munchies, take your pick,
Giggles linger, what a trick!

Sprinkles rain down like confetti,
These treats are far from petty,
With every bite, our giggles swell,
A feast of fun—we'll never tell!

So bring the honey, pour it on,
We'll sip and slurp until the dawn,
A playful end to every taste,
In our sweet world, there's no haste!

Brook of Pleasurable Sounds

In the kitchen, sounds abound,
Mixing laughter, bubbling sound,
Spoon clinks with a happy cheer,
Joyful songs as flavors near.

Drizzling honey like a dance,
Each drop holds a playful chance,
Whispers of delight arise,
With every taste, surprise, surprise!

Loud munching, crunching, what a spree,
Each bite's a tuneful jubilee,
Who knew snacks could be such fun?
A sweet duet for everyone!

So let us feast, let spirits rise,
With jolly jests and joyous sighs,
Our brook of sounds, a symphony,
In our kitchen, wild and free!

The Essence of Spring's Bounty

In the garden, blooms so bright,
Bees are buzzing with delight.
Flowers dance in sunny cheer,
Sticky sweetness drawing near.

With each sip, a giggle grows,
A bee in a hat, how it shows!
Petals painted in hues divine,
Oh, that pollen's hard to find!

Sipping sunshine, what a view,
Daffodils swaying, all askew.
Wiggly worms underfoot play,
Laughing at the mess we make!

Stumbling back, I miss my step,
Into a flower, what a rep!
The nectar's slippery as a song,
Spring's a circus, can't go wrong!

A Palette of Sugared Moments

Colors swirl like laughter bright,
With each bite, a pure delight.
Fruit and flower, dressed in cheer,
A rainbow snack, oh dear, oh dear!

I gobbled down a peachy treat,
Out jumped a frog, a funny feat!
"Save some for me!" he did croak,
As I had to stifle a joke.

Dancing pineapples, oh what fun,
Wiggling worms join in the run.
Skittles rain from apple trees,
Whispering secrets in the breeze.

Banana peels, they slip so sly,
Making everyone glide and fly.
Life's a feast, what a delight,
In this sugary, silly light!

Honeyed Secrets of Nature

Bees wear suits, they look so fine,
Gathering secrets, that honeyed line.
In the flowers, there's much to say,
Nature's giggles roll away.

Bumblebees play hopscotch, how odd,
Dancing on clovers, give 'em a nod!
Little critters, sharing their ways,
Life's a joke, on sunny days.

A honey jar laughed, it spilled on me,
Stuck in giggles, so sticky and free.
Got my friend, a hunky ant,
Pushing jam with his funny chant.

Nature's buffet, all on plate,
Worms tell jokes; oh, isn't fate great?
A funny twist in every sip,
Honey hugs with a happy quip!

Lush Drops of Memory

Lush drops falling, what a thrill,
A memory's treat that can't stay still.
Catch a dribble from the sky,
As whipped cream clouds flop by.

Laughing as the raindrops mix,
With splashes, twists, and funny tricks.
A splash of shimmer on my nose,
Nature's giggle, how it flows!

Bouncing berries in the breeze,
Jumping frogs call out with ease.
"Hop along, let's share a sip!"
As gummy worms do a funny flip.

Each drop shines like a painted grin,
With every chuckle, nature wins.
Memory's feast, what joy we glean,
In honeyed laughter, we convene!

Delight in Every Drop

I sat beneath a blooming tree,
With honey drips all over me.
I swatted flies, they danced around,
In my sticky throne, I softly frowned.

The bees were buzzing, quite a show,
They thought I was a flower, though!
I giggled as they stole my snack,
With every buzz, I felt a whack.

A mini feast on my warm face,
A sticky smile, oh, what a grace!
My friends all laughed, they couldn't see,
The syrupy joy that was in me.

So here's to sweet, delightful news,
A laugh is sweet when you choose to lose!
With every drop, my heart did hop,
In sticky bliss, I never stop!

Sweetness in the Air

A candy cloud floated by today,
I chased it down, come what may!
With every step, I tripped and fell,
Sticking to the ground—what a gel!

The butterflies were tickled pink,
As I slurped up a soda drink.
I wore a straw like a fancy hat,
While bees pushed on with a gentle pat.

A fruity scent swept through the breeze,
I danced around like a bumblebee.
But my feet got tangled in a vine,
And there I sat, oh, so divine!

Laughter bubbled, friends all near,
It seems sweet chaos brings such cheer.
With every giggle, my heart would flare,
In this funny, lovely, sugary air!

The Orchard's Lull

In an orchard packed with glee,
I tried to hug a peach tree—
But instead, it rained down fruits,
And there I stood in sticky boots!

My buddy laughed, he couldn't cope,
I turned, and saw the slippery slope.
We slid and slipped, like clowns in a show,
Fruits flying high, oh, what a blow!

The ground became our juicy stage,
Performing for bees—a funny age!
With every slip, we lost our pride,
But joy was rolling, with laughter as our guide.

So here we lay, in sweet delight,
Covered in fruit, just feeling right.
An orchard's lull, ol' summer's snack,
With goofy grins, there's no looking back!

Dreams of Juicy Days

Upon the green, I dreamt a line,
Of gummy bears and grape divine.
As I strolled through a marshmallow maze,
I knew I'd never leave this daze!

A soda fountain, oh what a sight,
I dove right in, what pure delight!
With every splash, I felt like a kid,
A fizzy boom—whoops! There I hid!

Cotton candy clung around my hair,
A sticky crown—how could I care?
Life's too sweet to worry or fret,
Beneath the sun, no regrets are met.

So raise your glass to this fine spree,
A world of fun, just come and see!
With juicy dreams, let laughter play,
And dance with joy through every day!

The Essence of Warmth

In a cup that giggles bright,
Lemon drops in joyful flight,
Sugar swirls like dancing sprites,
Chasing shadows, day and night.

Lemonade on a summer spree,
Sipping sunshine, wild and free,
Honeybees buzz merrily,
Sweetness drips, oh woe is me!

Here comes joy, in colors bold,
With every sip, a tale unfolds,
Grapefruit whispers secrets told,
Like best friends in warmest fold.

Fuzzy peaches prance about,
In the jar, they flip and flout,
Who knew giggles could pop out?
Joy in fruit, that's what it's about!

Elysian Sips

In whimsical clouds, fluids play,
Fruits collide in sweet ballet,
Sipping dreams, we drift away,
Giggling as we swish and sway.

A mango mischief joins the fun,
Pineapple frowns, "Oh, are we done?"
Lime spins tales that weigh a ton,
While raspberries giggle in the sun.

Berry patches start to cheer,
They lob their juice without a fear,
A toast to joy, let's all revere,
The playful sips that bring us near.

In glasses raised with raucous cheer,
Fruits tease each other, never peer,
Come join the laughter, all is clear,
Elysian moments, year by year!

Liquid Sunshine

Dripping gold with a silly grin,
Each splash and giggle pulls you in,
Chasing clouds on a paper thin,
Who knew fun and drink could spin?

Like a party with bubbles galore,
Juicy giggles, who could want more?
Crunchy apples shake the floor,
Dance with oranges, explore!

Bananas swing, hang on tight,
Juices splash with sheer delight,
One small sip, and you take flight,
Search for fizz in the moonlight.

Every gulp's a sunny jest,
With friends beside, we feel so blessed,
Liquid rays, we can't contest,
In this cheer, we find our rest!

Moments of Opalescence

A blend of hues, what a sight!
In tall glasses, colors ignite,
Laughter bubbles, spirits light,
Every sip, pure delight!

Papaya flirts with vibrant flair,
Mint joins in with a spicy dare,
Tasting joy is beyond compare,
Let's share this refreshing air.

Glints of joy in every drop,
Fruit parade that simply won't stop,
Time to celebrate and swap,
In this nectar, we can't plop!

Euphoria dances, laughter flows,
In a world where everyone knows,
Life's a jest that brightly glows,
With each sip, adventure grows!

Delicate Sweetness in the Breeze

In the garden, bees do prance,
With blossoms dressed, they take their chance.
Each flower whispers, 'Come, find me!'
Buzzing tunes in harmony.

Little ants in a parade,
Under the sun, they dance, unafraid.
They raise a toast with tiny feet,
Gathering treasures, oh so sweet!

A drop of sunshine, a breezy wink,
Flavors collide, oh what a stink!
One taste makes them cartwheel,
Laughing loudly, what a deal!

Sipping whispers from petals round,
A giggle here, a chuckle found.
Nature's candies make them grin,
In the garden, where fun begins!

Elixir of the Evening Glow

As daylight fades, the critters cheer,
Crickets sing, and shed their fear.
Fireflies swirl like sparkling wine,
Joining the dance, oh, how divine!

With bowls of nectar, the frogs all sing,
Hopping around, they embrace the spring.
A sip of joy from a lily's cup,
In the twilight, they never give up!

Moths flutter 'round, what a blunder!
Lip-smacking delights, an evening wonder.
They trip and slip on their own bling,
In dusk's embrace, they all take wing.

With laughter echoing in the light,
The party rages, amigos in flight.
A toast to the night, let good times flow,
In the sweet air, where fun will grow!

Drips of Joy from Petal's Edge

A droplet glimmers like a lost gem,
Sipping slowly from a flower's hem.
Ladybugs giggle as they scurry fast,
Like itsy bitsy cars, they zoom and blast.

The butterflies prance, waving their wings,
Drawing crowds as they do silly things.
A taste of laughter from each bloom,
What's sweeter than a flower's perfume?

Sipping the dew in morning light,
Even snails are having a bite.
Sliding slow with a shell on back,
Wonders of nectar—oh, what a snack!

The sun rolls high, they can't keep still,
Nature's playground, a thrill to fulfill.
Caterpillars tumble, spin, and dive,
In this wild joy, they're truly alive!

Vivid Sips from Nature's Cup

With a cheerful hum, the bees descend,
Creating laughter around each bend.
Bumblebees buzz with comedic flair,
Finding a sip, oh, what a pair!

Grasshoppers leap, a flying treat,
Joining the feast in the summer heat.
They play hopscotch on leaves so bright,
Nectar-filled laughter, pure delight!

The taste of blooms brings breezy cheer,
Twirling along, they all appear.
A sticky surprise from a clumsy pixie,
Falling in comically, oh how risky!

With each sip, all worries drift,
Nature's humor is the ultimate gift.
They caper and giggle, a joyful ruckus,
In this vibrant cup, nothing can stop us!

Nectar of the Ancients

In a jar marked 'Do Not Touch',
A strange goo sits in a clutch.
Old folks say it's a delight,
But it smells like a cat's plight.

I scooped a spoonful, oh what bliss,
Flew back ten feet with a twisty twist.
Ancient flavors danced and pranced,
Now I question my culinary stance.

They say it sparks joy and mirth,
But I learned what's of real worth.
Next time I'll just take a sip,
From that old, juicy, fruit-filled lip.

With a grin and my face full cheer,
I chased those bees around here.
They say the real pot of gold,
Is having fun when you're old.

Golden Kisses

In the garden, bees go nuts,
In search of sweetness from their ruts.
A buzzing choir, they take their flight,
To give gold hugs, oh what a sight!

I tried to steal a taste so fine,
But they chased me like a cussin' line.
Nectar drops sparkled in the sun,
Made me giggle, oh what fun!

I offered cookies, they took a whiff,
A tiny swarm and then a lift.
I ran, arms flailing with delight,
Who knew bees could start a fight?

But in the end, we shared some joy,
A sticky mess, oh what a ploy!
Golden kisses on my nose,
A sweet reminder where laughter grows.

Nature's Sweet Serenade

A tree once sang a gushy tune,
Swaying branches, a sweet cartoon.
Critters danced in pure delight,
As nectar dripped, what a sight!

I grabbed a cup to catch the flow,
But ended up with sticky dough.
Sipped and slurped, like a kid in bliss,
Even ants joined, how could I miss?

They couldn't resist this luscious pool,
While I tried acting all so cool.
But soon my shirt was a gooey mess,
Nature laughed, I must confess.

Amidst the laughter, joy was spread,
With bees as guests, fear fled.
A sweet serenade in the breeze,
Life's a laugh, just like these trees.

Surreal Flavors

In dreamland, I found a snack,
A rainbow bowl with a curious knack.
Sips of fluff and bites of fun,
Surreal flavors just begun!

I swallowed one, then burst with glee,
I saw a giraffe dance with me.
Candy clouds, oh what a treat,
Everything here tasted sweet!

A pickle cat with wings spread wide,
Offered a hint of buttery slide.
I laughed aloud, oh what a whirl,
In this bizarre, funny world.

But when I woke, what a shock,
My kitchen was full of mock.
A taste of whimsy, that's for sure,
In dreams, don't forget to explore!

Elixirs of the Soul

In a jar labeled 'do not touch,'
A mix of giggles and such.
A sip sends folks on a ride,
With wobbly feet and eyes open wide.

"Is it pickle juice or sweet jam?"
We laugh and debate—oh, what a sham!
The flavor bursts, a crazy dance,
We spill our drinks, but who needs a chance?

The blueberry twang, a silly flip,
One taste and you need a napkin tip.
Belly laughs blend with each sip,
What a delight, what a fun trip!

In this bizarre world of brewed delight,
Mirth is the potion that feels just right.
Pouring fun into cups, we sigh,
Chasing laughter and nectar, oh my!

Transcendent Honeycombs

In a garden where gummy bears bloom,
We trip on daffodils, oh the doom!
With flavors fighting to be the best,
We take a bite, put our taste buds to the test.

The bees all giggle, forming a band,
Playing sweet tunes, oh so grand.
Pollen jokes flying in the air,
Buzzing laughter—beyond compare!

A drizzle of syrup, oh what a tease,
We stick to our chairs, struggling to please.
Sipping concoctions, a sugary tide,
Our giggles multiply with every ride.

A sticky affair, our tongues in a twist,
Who knew a honeycomb could be such a mist?
Laughing through flavors, we soar on high,
In this whimsical world, just you and I!

Palette of Bliss

A rainbow on a plate, what a sight!
With mashed-up colors, oh, what a flight.
Scoops of ice cream dance around,
While whipped cream mountains tumble down.

Strawberry polka dots get stuck in hair,
Splatters of chocolate everywhere!
We play with spoons like it's a game,
Waging war in the name of "flavor fame."

Each bite's a hiccup, a splendid surprise,
We're artists, creators in sweet disguise.
Painting our tastes in swirls and swokes,
Giggling at the mess, oh how it provokes!

Finishing the canvas, we bow and cheer,
A masterpiece savored, joy sincere.
Our palette a riot, our laughter's the key,
In a world of flavors, just you and me!

Soft Hues of Flavor

A cupcake throne, where dreams do sit,
With frosting clouds, how can we quit?
Sprinkles rain like a party parade,
Our giggles echo, sweet memories made.

Biting into fluff, the joy ignites,
Sugar rush soaring like dazzling kites.
We tumble and roll, in this edible bliss,
Taking selfies, can you believe this?

Cupcake crumbs? They're just confetti!
We laugh and argue, 'Is it too heavy?'
With every bite, our worries dissolve,
In this kingdom of sugar, sweet chaos evolves.

So dig in deep, let's chase a delight,
In this frosted paradise, everything's bright.
With soft hues of flavor, we hum as we play,
In a sugary world where we laugh all day!

Sunlit Harvest

Bumblebees buzz in the sun,
Honey drips, oh what fun!
A dance with flowers, what a sight,
Sticky fingers, pure delight.

Lemonade spills down the slide,
We laugh as we take a ride.
Watermelons make a splash,
Juicy bites gone in a flash.

Picnic ants march in a row,
Sneaky thieves, they steal the show.
Jars of jam stacked to the brim,
On toast, they make our faces grin.

In the orchard, laughter rings,
As we munch on all good things.
Sunshine smiles, the sky's so blue,
Harvest time brings joy anew.

Forbidden Delights

Chocolate rivers, oh so deep,
Silly dreams that make us leap.
Frosting fights and cherry wars,
Sticky hugs and open doors.

Whipped cream mountains, pure and white,
Cakes that soar to dizzy heights.
Sneaky spoon, don't get caught,
In the pantry, we'll get fraught.

Candy lands, a twisted path,
Where giggles grow and mischief hath.
Gummy bears and licorice trees,
Sugar sprites dancing on the breeze.

Undercover taste parade,
Sipping treats that sweetly fade.
Forbidden fun, we can't resist,
Every bite, a tasty twist.

Nectarous Paths

Wobbly jelly on the floor,
A colorful, bouncing floor.
Marshmallow clouds float above,
In our world of gooey love.

Trail of sprinkles leads the way,
To a land where giggles play.
Candy canes that line the street,
Walking barefoot feels so sweet.

Lollipop forests, oh so bright,
Swirling colors in the light.
Chocolate rivers all around,
Silly laughter is the sound.

Every step a squishy squeeze,
Honey drizzles bring us ease.
Nectar springs, we leap and laugh,
Taste a slice of joy's sweet graph.

A Tapestry of Taste

Doughnuts hanging from the trees,
Lemon zest riding a breeze.
Taste buds dance, they jump for joy,
Flavors swirl, oh what a ploy!

Pizza pies float in the air,
Cheesy smiles, without a care.
Pickles flying with delight,
Crunching sounds a scrumptious sight.

Bubbly soda, fizzy fun,
Cupcake castles, oh what a run.
With every bite, we giggle more,
Creativity, we can't ignore.

A cheer for snacks we hold so tight,
A colorful canvas, pure delight.
In this feast, we laugh and play,
A tapestry of taste, hooray!

Vines of Velvet

In a garden where giggles grow,
Grapes wear hats like pros in a show.
They dance on vines, a silly parade,
With juicy tales of fruit escapade.

A squirrel in shades tries to steal the scene,
While bees wear ties, they're looking quite keen.
A fumble, a tumble, oh what a sight,
As cherries roll away, taking flight!

Laughter bubbles where the sunshine beams,
As watermelon ducks float down in streams.
The vines of velvet twist and twine,
Creating a party; oh, how divine!

With every bite, a giggle bursts,
A flavor explosion, oh, how it thirsts!
So join the fun, don't miss the cheer,
In the fruity carnival, let's all appear!

Melodies of Flavor

In a fruit bowl band, the apples strum,
While oranges tango, oh what a hum!
The bananas slide in a peel-out race,
Making silly noises, oh, sweet embrace.

The grapes start singing, a high-pitched tune,
Jamming with berries under the moon.
A raspberry winks, oh what a tease,
As honey drips down with the greatest of ease.

Together they play in a colorful mix,
Each flavor a note, playing tricks.
With laughter so bright, and a fruity flare,
The melodies surround us; they fill the air!

So grab your fork and join the fun,
In this fruity symphony, we'll never run.
A harmony of giggles, sweet and pure,
Where every bite makes our laughter endure!

Luscious Secrets

A pineapple wearing a mischievous grin,
Hiding sweet secrets tucked deep within.
While berries plot behind leafy screens,
Whispering tales of wild, juicy schemes.

A fig in a mask claims to be quite shy,
Yet rolls down the hill, oh my, oh my!
Peaches giggle, their fuzz all aflame,
As they create chaos, no one's to blame.

In the secret garden where fun is a game,
Riddles in fruit, oh what a claim!
The flavors surprise, they dance and they flip,
In this wild world, we all take a sip!

So come, take a dive into luscious delight,
Where humor and fruit bring joy to the night.
A banquet of laughter, secrets revealed,
In this zany land, we're all sealed!

Sun-Soaked Lullabies

Under the sun, fruits sing soft tunes,
Plum fairies twirl with wise old raccoons.
Watermelons lounging on golden sand,
Sipping on sunshine, isn't it grand?

Apricots giggle, wrapped in dreams,
As nectar drips down in sweet, sticky streams.
Pineapples grin like they know a joke,
While cherries toss seeds, oh what a poke!

The breeze brings whispers of fun and cheer,
As fruit folk gather, we celebrate here.
With laughter so bright, it echoes along,
In this sun-soaked lullaby, we all belong!

So join the chorus, let humor collide,
With fruit-filled adventures, let's take a ride.
In every juicy laugh, and sunbeam so sly,
We find our magic beneath the blue sky!